21st Century
Basic Skills
Library

PUPPIES GROW UP TO BE DOGS

by Cecilia Minden, PhD

Cherry Lake Publishing • Ann Arbor, Michigan

1

Published in the United States of America
by Cherry Lake Publishing
Ann Arbor, Michigan
www.cherrylakepublishing.com

Photo Credits: Cover and page 1, ©Pack-Shot/Shutterstock, Inc.; page 4,
©Joy Brown/Shutterstock, Inc.; page 6, ©poutnik/Shutterstock, Inc.;
page 8, ©Close Encounters Photography/Shutterstock, Inc.; page 10,
©Ursula/Shutterstock, Inc.; page 12, ©aleksandar zoric/Shutterstock, Inc.;
page 14, ©Monika Wisniewska/Shutterstock, Inc.; page 16, ©beltsazar/
Shutterstock, Inc.; page 18, ©vgm/Shutterstock, Inc.; page 20, ©Jeff
Dalton/Shutterstock, Inc.

Library of Congress Cataloging-in-Publication Data
Minden, Cecilia.
  Puppies grow up to be dogs/by Cecilia Minden.
      p. cm.—(21st century basic skills library. Level 1)
  Includes bibliographical references and index.
  ISBN-13: 978-1-60279-851-9 (lib. bdg.)
  ISBN-10: 1-60279-851-6 (lib. bdg.)
  1. Puppies—Juvenile literature. I. Title. II. Series.
  SF426.5.M574 2010
  636.7'07—dc22   2009048596

Cherry Lake Publishing would like to acknowledge
the work of The Partnership for 21st Century Skills.
Please visit *www.21stcenturyskills.org* for more information.

Printed in the United States of America
Corporate Graphics Inc.
July 2010
CLFA07

TABLE OF CONTENTS

5 Puppies

15 Growing Up

21 Dogs

22 Find Out More

22 Glossary

23 Home and School Connection

24 Index

24 About the Author

Puppies

Puppies are baby dogs.

They are born in **litters**.

Puppies are small.

They take a lot of naps.

Puppies like to **cuddle**.

They feel safe and warm.

Puppies cannot see or hear when they are small.

Puppies **nurse** their mother's milk.

Growing Up

Puppies eat food when they get bigger.

Puppies like to run and play.

They like to chew!

Puppies need clean water and food.

Be **gentle** when you pet them.

Dogs

At 2 years old, puppies are all grown up.

They will always like to play!

Find Out More

BOOK

Minden, Cecilia. *Farm Animals: Dogs*. Ann Arbor, MI: Cherry Lake
  Publishing, 2009.

WEB SITE

Top 10 Best Family Dogs
animal.discovery.com/videos/top-10-family-dogs/
Watch videos about the top 10 dogs for families.

Glossary

cuddle (KUH-duhl) to lie closely together for comfort or warmth

gentle (JEN-tul) soft

litters (LIT-urz) groups of baby animals born at the same time to
the same mother

nurse (NURSS) to drink milk from one's mother

Home and School Connection

Use this list of words from the book to help your child become a better reader. Word games and writing activities can help beginning readers reinforce literacy skills.

a	dogs	mother's	take
all	eat	naps	their
always	feel	need	them
and	food	nurse	they
are	gentle	of	to
at	get	old	up
baby	growing	or	warm
be	grown	pet	water
bigger	hear	play	when
born	in	puppies	will
cannot	like	run	years
chew	litters	safe	you
clean	lot	see	
cuddle	milk	small	

Index

chewing, 17
cuddling, 9

dogs, 5, 21

food, 15, 19

gentleness, 19

hearing, 11

litters, 5

milk, 13

naps, 7
nursing, 13

playing, 17, 21

running, 17

safety, 9
seeing, 11
size, 7

warmth, 9
water, 19

About the Author

Cecilia Minden is the former Director of the Language and Literacy Program at the Harvard Graduate School of Education. She currently works as a literacy consultant for school and library publishers and is the author of more than 100 books for children.

24